STEAMTEAM 5 ™

THE BEGINNING
COLORING & ACTIVITY BOOK

STEAMTEAM5.com

Be sure to follow this book series on www.STEAMTeam5.com.

ISBN-978-0-9993187-1-3

Printed in the U.S.A.

Color STEAMTEAM™ 5

In this scene, STEAMTEAM 5 sets out to search for someone very special.

SANDIA SCIENTIST

KREBS CYCLE

_____, **the Astronaut**

Finish this drawing to make yourself an astronaut!

Weather Words

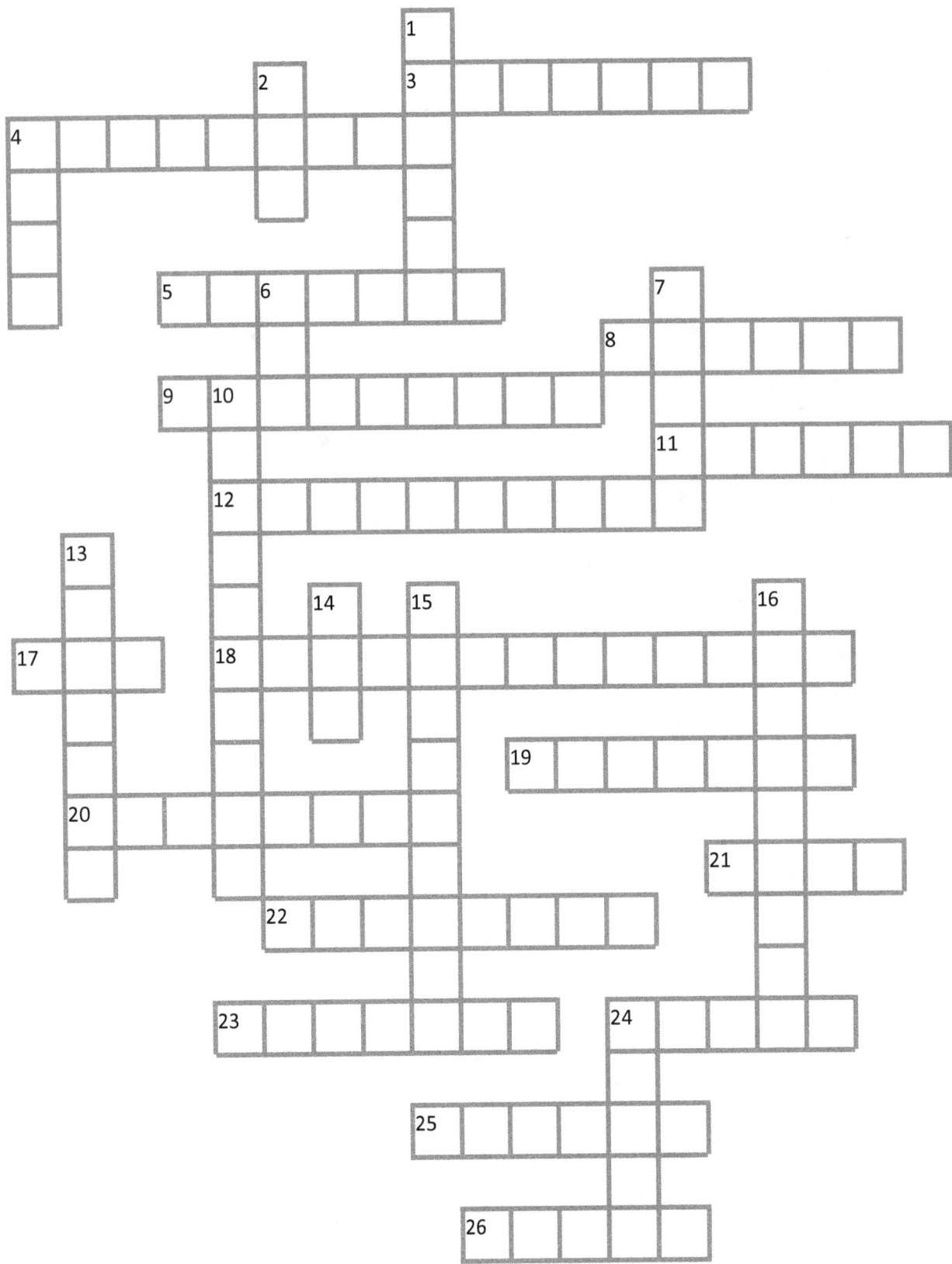

AIR
ATMOSPHERE
BAROMETER
BREEZE
CLIMATE
CLOUDS

CONTRAILS
DEW
DROUGHT
EROSION
FLOOD
FOG

FREEZE
FRONT
FROST
GLACIER
HAIL
HAZE

HUMIDITY
HURRICANE
ICE
LIGHTNING
MICROBURST
MONSOON

NIMBUS
OVERCAST
PRECIPITATION
RAINBOW

	Across		Down
3.	Caused by the reflection and refraction (bending) of sunlight passing through raindrops.	1.	Occurs when the temperature falls below 32 degrees over a large area for an extended period of time.
4.	Intense storms with swirling winds up to 150 miles per hour.	2.	A water substance in the solid phase.
5.	A large piece of ice that survives for many years, slowly carving out the face of earth.	4.	Tiny particles of dust, smoke, salt or pollution droplets that are scattered through the air.
8.	A light wind.	6.	The mixture of gases that form the atmosphere of the Earth.
9.	An instrument that measures air pressure.	7.	A boundary between two different air masses, resulting in stormy weather.
11.	The Latin word for "rain" used to describe a cloud or group of clouds from which rain falls.	10.	A layer of gases surrounding a planet.
12.	A small downdraft of air with an outflow diameter of less than 2.5 miles with the peak winds lasting from 2 to 5 minutes.	13.	The wearing away of the Earth's surface by the action of the sea, running water, moving ice, precipitation or wind.
17.	A cloud on the ground that reduces visibility.	14.	Water that forms on objects close to the ground when its temperature falls below the dew point of the surface air.
18.	Rain, snow, sleet, or hail that falls to the ground.	15.	A very bright flash of electricity that happens in a thunderstorm.
19.	The average weather conditions in a certain place or during a certain season.	16.	Long, narrow, ice-crystal clouds that form behind jet planes flying at high altitudes in below-freezing temperatures.
20.	When a layer of clouds covers all of the sky.	24.	Caused by days of heavy rain and/or melting snows, when rivers rise and go over their banks.
21.	A mixture of liquid and frozen precipitation.		
22.	The amount of water vapor in the air.		
23.	A period when a region has a lack of rainfall.		
24.	White ice crystals that form on a surface, like the ground or leaves of a plant		
25.	A seasonal wind that reverses direction between summer and winter and often brings heavy rains.		
26.	A visible collection of tiny water droplets or, at colder temperatures, ice crystals floating in the air above the surface.		

Parts of a Flower

```
            L Z Z
          A A F Q C
          N T U S D
      F D N E Q M S     S T
    U X D F   P C G   A G G C
    V Y G H I I S T A M E N P
    T N E M A L I F Y H R W Q
      T I M   M A O   O L M
          E   F S J V
      O S T E M T T B O G M
      K W S R   Y   D X A V
      R T H U   L   E Y W O
        V U     L     T N
                E
                S
                E
                E
                V
                H
                L
                S
                R
    I L S O A N T H E R F F I
      I E N T A H D H D D F
      T P B T M S I Y P H M
      S A W S G H W R E Q Q
      I L P C I E I A J K M
      P M C J T G B V D H O
        C J W S V E O S A
        D R P T U L H S M
```

ANTHER   PETAL   STAMEN   STYLE
FILAMENT   PISTIL   STEM
OVARY   SEPAL   STIGMA

See how these parts work:

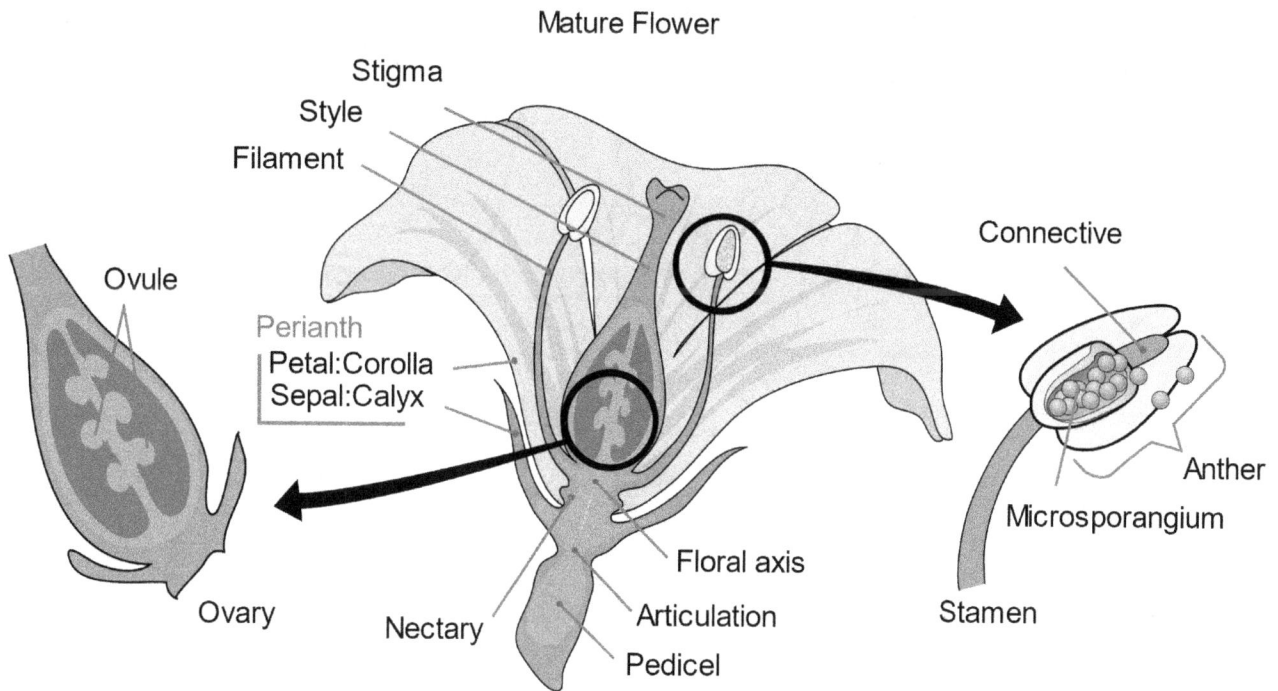

Mature Flower

Stigma
Style
Filament

Ovule

Perianth
Petal:Corolla
Sepal:Calyx

Connective

Anther

Microsporangium

Floral axis

Articulation

Pedicel

Ovary

Nectary

Stamen

Help this space traveler find her way back to her vehicle!

At the Science Fair

De-scramble each word to decrypt the final message.

TOEHYHSISP   ☐☐☐☐☐☐☐☐☐☐
  3   14

SEAMARTIL   ☐☐☐☐☐☐☐☐☐
  7

EGNISD   ☐☐☐☐☐☐
  9

TEPNIMERXE   ☐☐☐☐☐☐☐☐☐☐
  2

DISK   ☐☐☐☐
  1

RECSAHRE   ☐☐☐☐☐☐☐☐
  5

TEPSS   ☐☐☐☐☐
  4

LEAZYAN   ☐☐☐☐☐☐☐
  8

SIONLNUOCC   ☐☐☐☐☐☐☐☐☐☐
  6

SUSTELR   ☐☐☐☐☐☐☐
  10

TEOMDH

| | | | | | |
13

PUOSEPR

| | | | | | | |
12

ROEPERCUD

| | | | | | | | | |
15

TIESVBONRASO

| | | | | | | | | | | |
11

RCNESFEREE

| | | | | | | | | | |
16

STET

| | | | |
17

Decrypt the Message

| 1 | 2 | 3 | 4 |

| 5 | 6 | 1 | 7 | 8 | 9 |

| Q | | | | | | | | | |
| | 10 | 11 | 12 | 13 | 14 | 15 | 16 | 17 |

If you get stuck, hold this page facing a mirror to reveal the answer below:

Keep Asking Questions

TREEKA
TECHNOLOGIST

Who Doesn't Love Pizza?!

Draw a pciture of a pizza (remember to include your favorite toppings to this pizza!), then draw lines to show how you would cut it to serve 8 people.

Congrats! You just won this personal robot at the state fair! Name and decorate it to make it your own.

Make a list of chores you'd like to program your new robot to do for you.

I'll Program My New Robot to:

_____

_____

_____

_____

_____

_____

_____

_____

Technology Terms

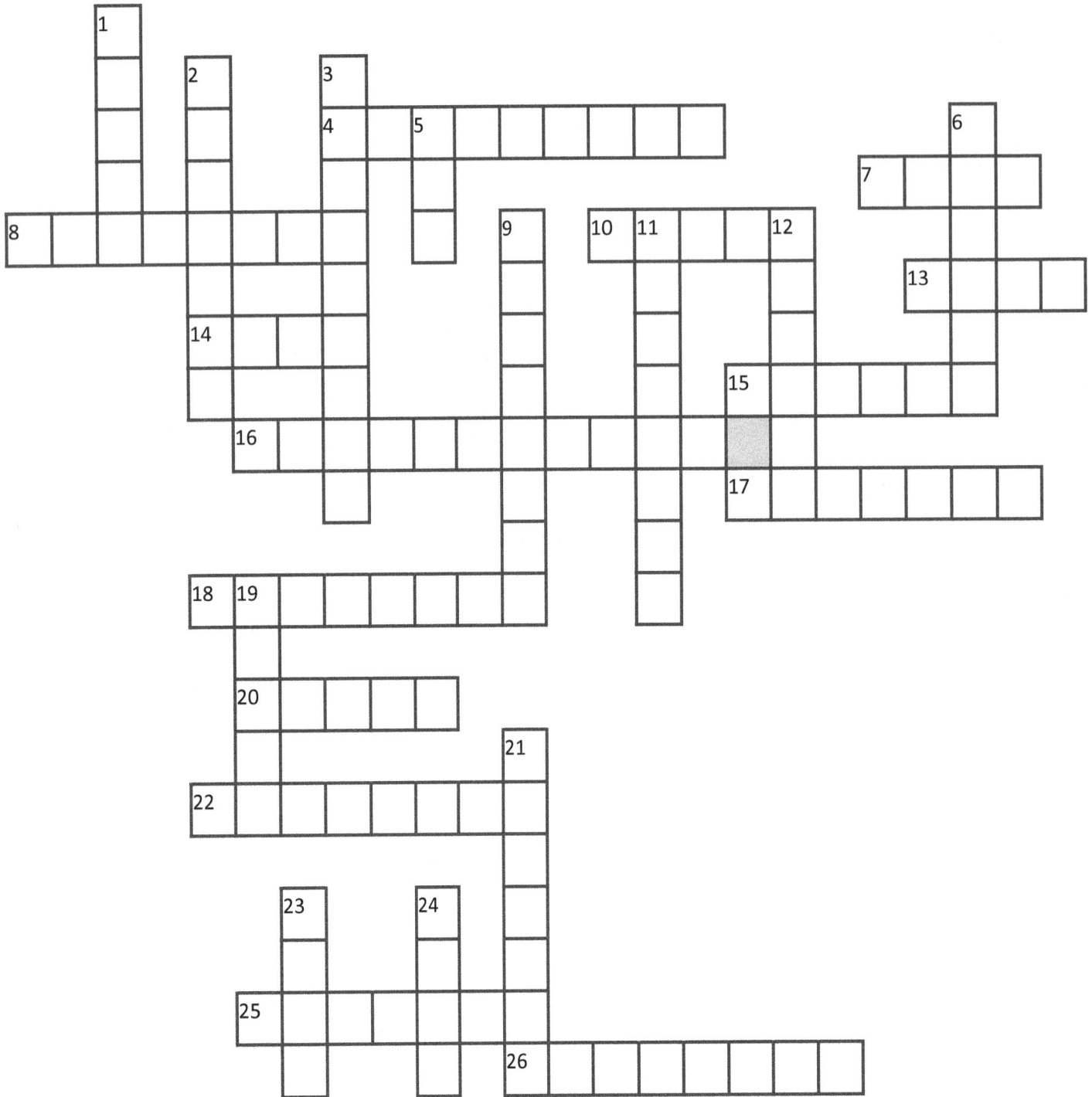

ALGORITHM
AUDIO
BANDWIDTH
BINARY
BROWSER
BYTE
CHIP

DATA
DATABASE
DRONE
EMAIL
GPS
GRAPHIC
HARDWARE

ICON
INTERNET
KEYBOARD
LINEAR
MEMORY
MONITOR
MOTHERBOARD

NETWORK
PASSWORD
PIXEL
SOFTWARE
VIRUS

	Across		Down
4.	A list of steps that you can follow to finish a task.	1.	A program created to steal or damage information on a computer.
7.	A tiny piece of silicon that has electronic circuits on it.	2.	A software program that is used to explore the Internet.
8.	A secret code used to prevent others to access a computer or computer program.	3.	A measure of how much data you can move through an Internet connection in a given amount of time.
10.	A tiny area of illumination on a computer's monitor.	5.	A space-based satellite navigation system that provides location and time information anywhere on or near the Earth.
13.	A collection of information.	6.	A way of counting using only the numbers 1 and 0
14.	Sending messages from one person to another over the Internet.	9.	A collection of data that is organized in a way that makes it easy for someone to access the information inside in various ways.
15.	The temporary storage of information on a computer.	11.	Millions of computers around the world connected together.
16.	The main electronic circuit board in a computer. It connects all of the system hardware.	12.	Moving in a straight line or path.
17.	An images or picture that is created, edited, and/or published using a computer.	19.	Relating to sound or its reproduction of sound.
18.	All of the physical components that make up a computer.	21.	A system of connected computers that allows the sharing of files and equipment.
20.	Also known as an unmanned aerial vehicle (UAV), it is an aircraft without a pilot on board.	23.	A picture that represents a file, folder or program on a computer.
22.	A set of instructions that tells the computer what to do.	24.	A string of bits that usually is eight bits in length. Each one contains coded information that represents various letters, words or phrases to a computer.
25.	A display screen used to provide visual output from a computer, video camera, drone controller, or other video generating device.		
26.	A set of keys or buttons used to type information into a computer.		

Space Travel

```
            I  L  T  V  L  Q  E  G
         K  V  U  U  Q  E  J  F  P  X  R  M
         W  F  N  A  R  H  K  X  J  L  U  P  E  W
      Z  J  A  N  O  C  A  P  S  U  L  E  J  L  V  S
   A  A  R  O  C  R  M  A  R  T  I  A  N  H  C  O  O  M
   P  P  R  K  K  S  S  M  U  O  R  B  I  T  E  R  R  R
P  I  T  E  P  O  A  L  P  X  T  K  S  E  P  L  A  N  E  T
L  S  T  W  A  I  G  K  L  A  W  E  C  A  P  S  C  Y  H  R
A  N  Y  P  Y  G  H  V  N  N  C  M  M  H  T  L  R  Z  Y  I
U  O  S  O  L  X  E  S  H  S  P  E  S  R  E  V  I  N  U  H
N  I  P  D  O  M  J  P  E  E  N  I  S  R  Y  I  Z  T  W  T
C  S  I  G  A  L  A  X  Y  C  F  E  L  U  J  D  M  N  H  A
H  S  W  T  D  J  H  N  Z  J  A  E  I  K  I  O  V  R  Y  N
E  I  J  L  F  F  K  C  O  D  C  P  F  L  O  T  U  R  E  W
   M  T  Q  Q  Z  L  C  R  B  B  Z  S  N  A  S  T  C  A
      I  N  T  E  R  G  A  L  A  C  T  I  C  T  N  O  Q  H
         U  P  X  H  M  A  R  S  G  M  X  E  E  W  R  R
         A  E  R  O  S  P  A  C  E  R  E  W  E  Q
            E  X  R  X  P  I  H  S  R  A  T  S
            E  L  T  T  U  H  S  A
```

AEROSPACE	INTERGALACTIC	ORBITER	SHUTTLE
ALIENS	LAUNCH	PAYLOAD	SPACESHIP
ASTRONAUT	LUNAR	PLANET	SPACESUIT
CAPSULE	MARS	POD	SPACEWALK
DOCK	MARTIAN	REENTRY	STARSHIP
EXPLORER	MISSION	ROCKET	THRUSTER
GALAXY	MOON	ROVER	UNIVERSE

EVELYN
ENGINEER

Skateboarders

Add safety equipment to these skateboarders, then build them a ramp!

Seesaw, the Simple Machine

A *simple machine* is a mechanical device that enables you to change the direction or magnitude of a force. One example of a simple machine is a *lever*.

A lever is strong bar that is used to lift and move something heavy. The bar rests on a *fulcrum*; when you apply force on one end of the bar, you can move an object on the other end.

One example of a lever is a seesaw. Draw yourself on one end of the seesaw and a friend on the other. (Whose legs will be applying force and whose will be up in the air?)

Fulcrum

Bridges

A bridge is a structure designed to provide a path over a river, ravine, road, railroad, or other obstacle. Color this scene and show someone (or something) using the bridge.

Fulcrum

Now, draw your own bridge below.

Simple Machines

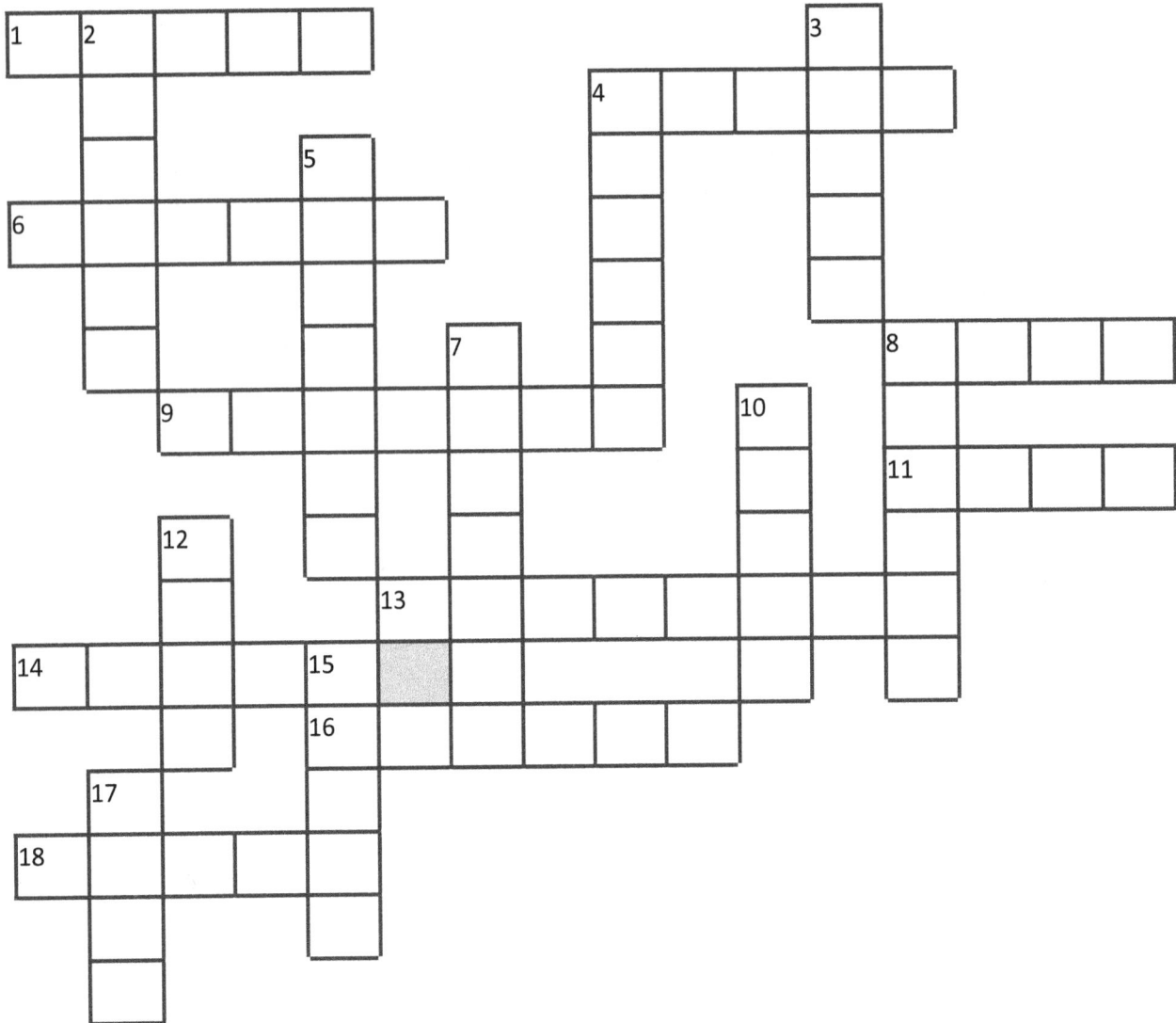

AXEL
DISTANCE
EFFORT
ENERGY
FORCE

FULCRUM
GEARS
LEVER
LOAD
MACHINE

PLANE
PULLEY
PUSH
SCREW
STAIRS

THREADS
TORQUE
WEDGE
WHEEL
WORK

	Across		Down
1.	Wheels with teeth.	2.	The force used to move an object.
4.	A type of simple machine that is found on a water bottle cap.	3.	A triangular shaped tool used to separate two objects or portions of an object, lift up an object, or hold an object in place.
6.	A force that causes rotation.	4.	People use this type of inclined plane to get to the second floor in their home.
8.	To move something away by pressing against it.	5.	The support in the middle of a seesaw is called a _____.
9.	A screw is made up of _____ wrapped around a post or rod.	7.	A tool that makes work easier.
11.	An object that is being moved.	8.	A wheel that is used with a cord or rope. When you pull it downward, the other end lifts upward.
13.	How far something is moved.	10.	An inclined _____ is a flat, slanted surface that works like a ramp.
14.	A round frame that turns on a pin or shaft in its middle.	12.	A bar on which a wheel turns.
16.	The ability to do work.	15.	A long tool such as a pole or a rod that is put under an object to lift it.
18.	A push or a pull.	17.	An effort in doing or making something.

There is no such thing as a child who hates to read; there are only children who have not found the right book. —Frank Serafini

ARIANA ARTIST

Symmetry

Symmetry means "the same on both sides." This butterfly shows an example of symmetry found in nature. Color the butterfly's wings so that they're symmetrical.

Is It a Tree?

Cognitive illusions demonstrate how the brain relates an image that we see to assumptions or knowledge that we already have. Below is a type of cognitive illusion called an *ambiguous illusion*, which is an image that can be perceived in more than one way.

Most people will see the tree, but can you also see the people in the image below?

Fibonacci Sequence

In mathematics, the Fibonacci sequence is a series of numbers in which each number equals the sum of the two numbers before it. It always starts with the numbers "0" and "1."

The sequence shown below is 0, 1, 1, 2, 3, 5, 8, 13, and 21.

So, after the first "0" and "1," the math looks like this:

0+1=1

1+1=2

1+2=3

2+3=5

3+5=8

5+8=13

8+13=21

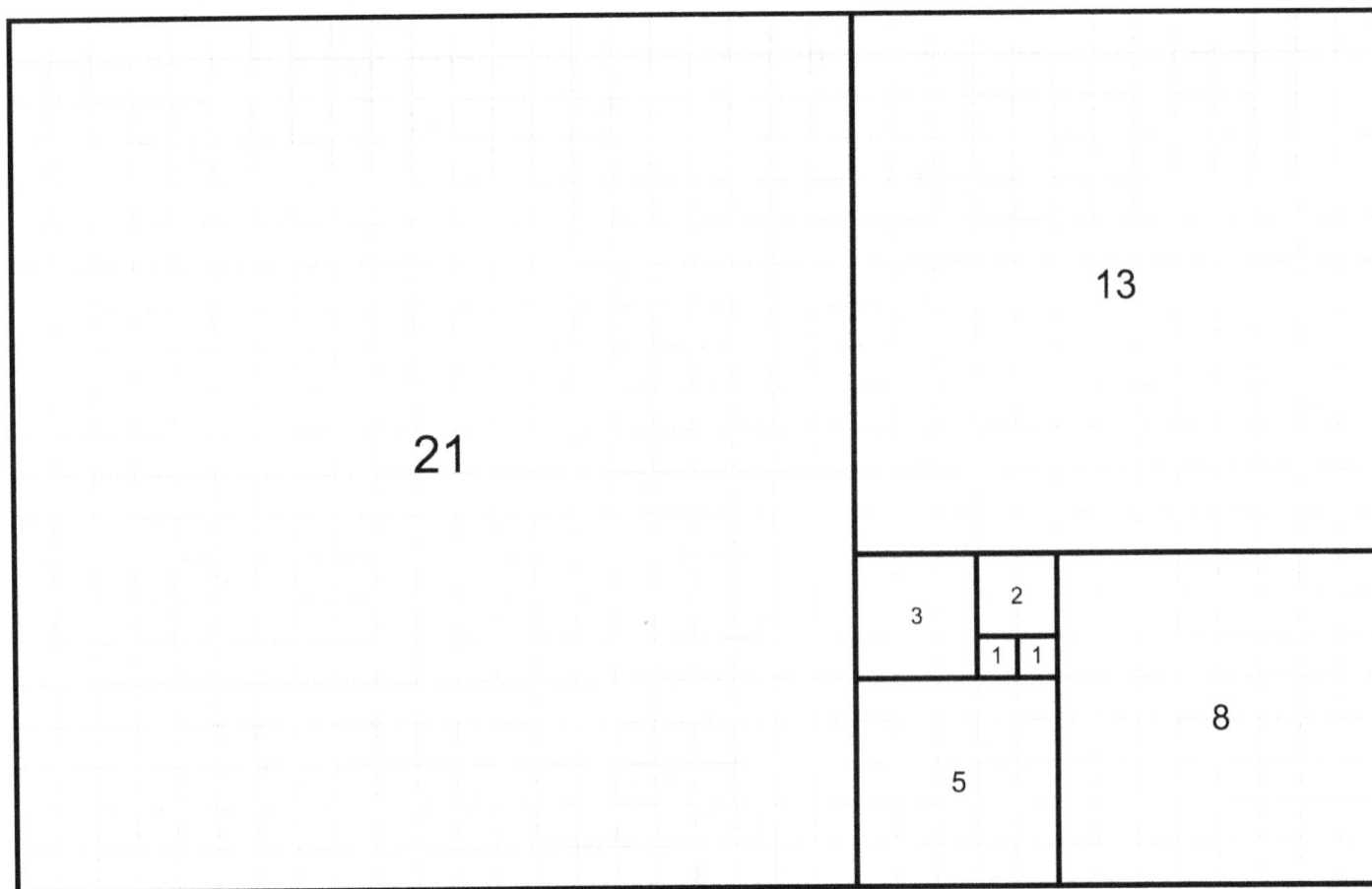

Fibonacci Sequence in Nature

This Nautilus shell is an example of Fibonacci's sequence, which is sometimes called the *Golden Spiral*. Notice that the spirals on this shell expand with every quarter, or 90 degree, turn from the center.

The chambers in this shell provide shelter for Nautilus, which are cephalopods. Ask a parent to help you look up photos of Nautilus online, then draw one of them using this shell as its home.

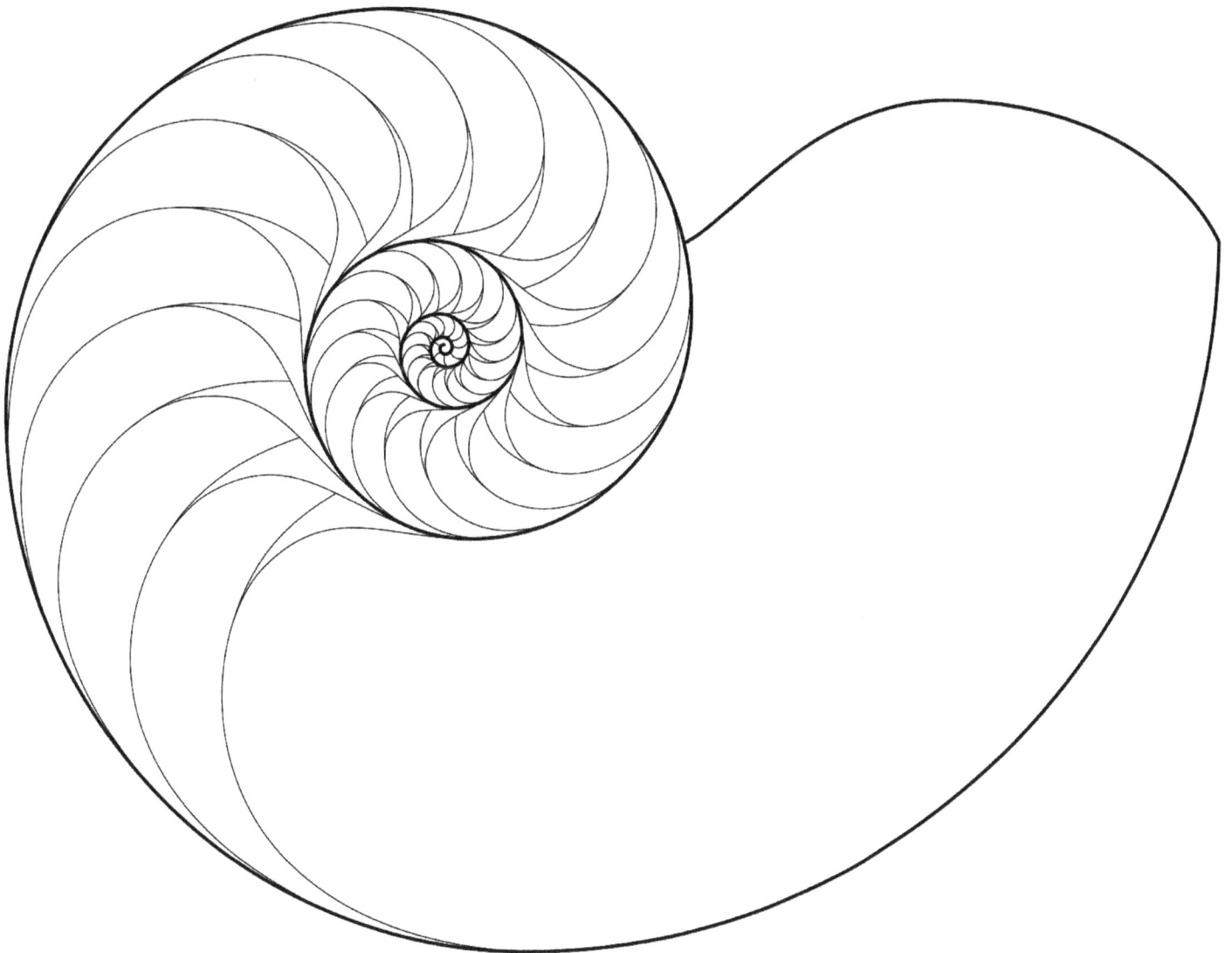

Color Me Artsy

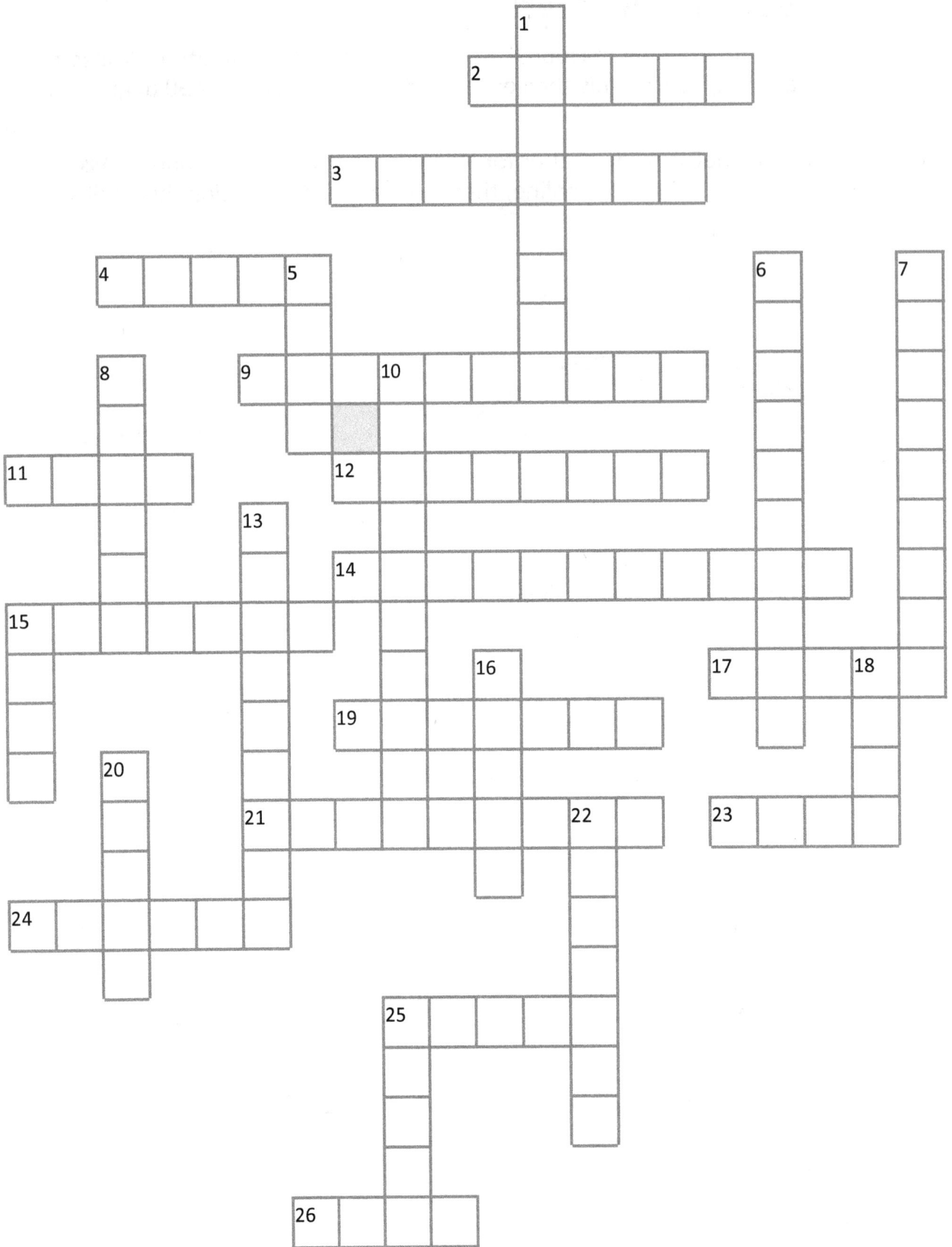

ANGLE
ARCHITECT
BACKGROUND
BLUE
CARVING
COLLAGE
COLUMN

COMPOSITION
CONTRAST
COOL
DARK
FORM
LANDSCAPE
LIFE

MATTE
MEDIA
MIRROR
MURAL
NEGATIVE
PHOTOGRAPHY
PORTRAIT

PROPORTION
RAINBOW
SCULPTURE
SOLID
STATUE
UNITY
VIEW

	Across		Down
2.	A supporting pillar on a building.	1.	This occurs when elements that are different are placed next to each other in a work of art.
3.	_____ space refers to the empty space between and surrounding shapes and forms.	5.	Value refers to how light or _____ a color is.
4.	A _____ line has no gaps or breaks in it.	6.	The part of a scene (or picture) that lies behind objects in the foreground.
9.	The relationship of the size of different objects to each other.	7.	Artwork that is three-dimensional and can be seen from all sides.
11.	Any object that has three dimensions (height, width, and depth).	8.	Symmetrical means that two sides of a work of art are _____ images of each other.
12.	A painting, drawing, or photograph of a person.	10.	A picture taken using a camera.
14.	The placement or arrangement of visual elements or ingredients in a work of art.	13.	A picture showing an area of countryside, nature, or land.
15.	Using tools to shape something from material by scraping away portions of that material.	15.	These types of colors are associated with things like snow, water, and grass.
17.	A shape formed when two lines extend in different directions from the same point.	16.	A feeling of belonging together.
19.	Neutral colors are colors that are not found in a _____.	18.	A picture of an arrangement of objects (for example, flowers or fruit) is called a still _____.
21.	Highly trained artists and engineers who design homes and buildings.	20.	A painting done on a wall.
23.	The three primary colors are red, yellow, and _____.	22.	Artwork that is created by cutting and pasting.
24.	Three-dimensional art that is in a body form.	25.	A visual texture that does not reflect much light.
25.	The materials and tools used by the artist to create a work of art.		
26.	Point of _____ refers to the position from which the viewer sees a work of art.		

Colors

De-scramble each word to decrypt the final message.

BEUL

9		8	

CBAKL

			1	

LODG

		12	

GEENR

	10			

AOGERN

7					

PELRUP

				3	

DER

LYELWO

				2	

WIHET

		11	17	

NIPK

[box, 4 cells]
14

RIVELS

[box, 6 cells]
13

RONWB

[box, 5 cells]
4

YGRE

[box, 4 cells]
6

LEAT

[box, 4 cells]
15

NADEELRV

[box, 8 cells]
5

NAMROO

[box, 6 cells]
16

[boxes 1 2 3 4 5] [boxes 6 7 8] [boxes 9 10 11 12 13 14 15 16 17] !

If you get stuck, hold this page facing a mirror to reveal the answer below:

Color You Brilliant!

MATTIE MATHEMATICIAN

Color you brilliant!

```
K  E  J  B  M  F  H  U  F  H  Q  N  E  W  G  K  J  F  C  I
H  S  J  C  C  H  K  F  D  B  M  J  S  D  P  V  D  Y  B  W
X  F  V  J  I  J  B  I  N  K  Q  U  Z  G  N  E  L  P  Z  A
H  M  F  S  H  R  M  I  R  B  N  L  E  N  U  I  A  L  P  N
O  H  F  K  N  A  C  G  Q  C  C  P  O  P  N  A  A  C  A  J
E  C  U  U  R  H  M  L  L  F  H  G  O  D  T  Z  M  U  R  L
P  P  S  Y  O  C  O  N  E  H  A  Y  E  W  T  G  Y  O  A  L
N  S  P  H  E  R  E  Y  J  X  R  R  R  A  R  S  O  D  L  I
R  O  K  S  M  J  M  Y  E  I  A  Q  B  P  A  E  E  U  L  O
E  H  G  F  I  C  W  H  E  U  T  Q  Y  L  P  P  R  Y  E  I
L  A  O  A  L  O  K  Y  J  W  S  S  F  R  E  J  A  S  L  W
G  Y  I  M  T  F  P  X  S  P  T  U  X  P  Z  R  U  A  O  F
N  Y  E  N  B  C  X  F  T  E  W  M  D  B  O  N  Q  I  G  Q
A  G  V  Z  X  U  O  N  Z  L  E  B  U  C  I  R  S  Y  R  P
I  M  D  B  A  D  S  K  N  B  K  A  O  N  D  C  O  F  A  V
R  I  Y  G  X  E  H  D  R  N  O  G  A  T  N  E  P  G  M  I
T  E  L  G  N  A  T  C  E  R  V  S  T  P  P  A  M  E  U  V
U  X  S  O  S  H  I  Q  V  D  T  N  S  O  O  Q  V  O  G  E
V  D  H  L  A  D  H  M  O  V  A  L  U  U  A  A  M  W  Z  B
J  D  O  O  Y  L  K  U  G  T  E  K  Z  M  E  L  Y  X  K  S
```

CIRCLE   OCTAGON   RECTANGLE   TRAPEZOID
CONE   OVAL   RHOMBUS   TRIANGLE
CUBE   PARALLELOGRAM   SPHERE
CYLINDER   PENTAGON   SQUARE
HEXAGON   PYRAMID   STAR

Math for the Masses

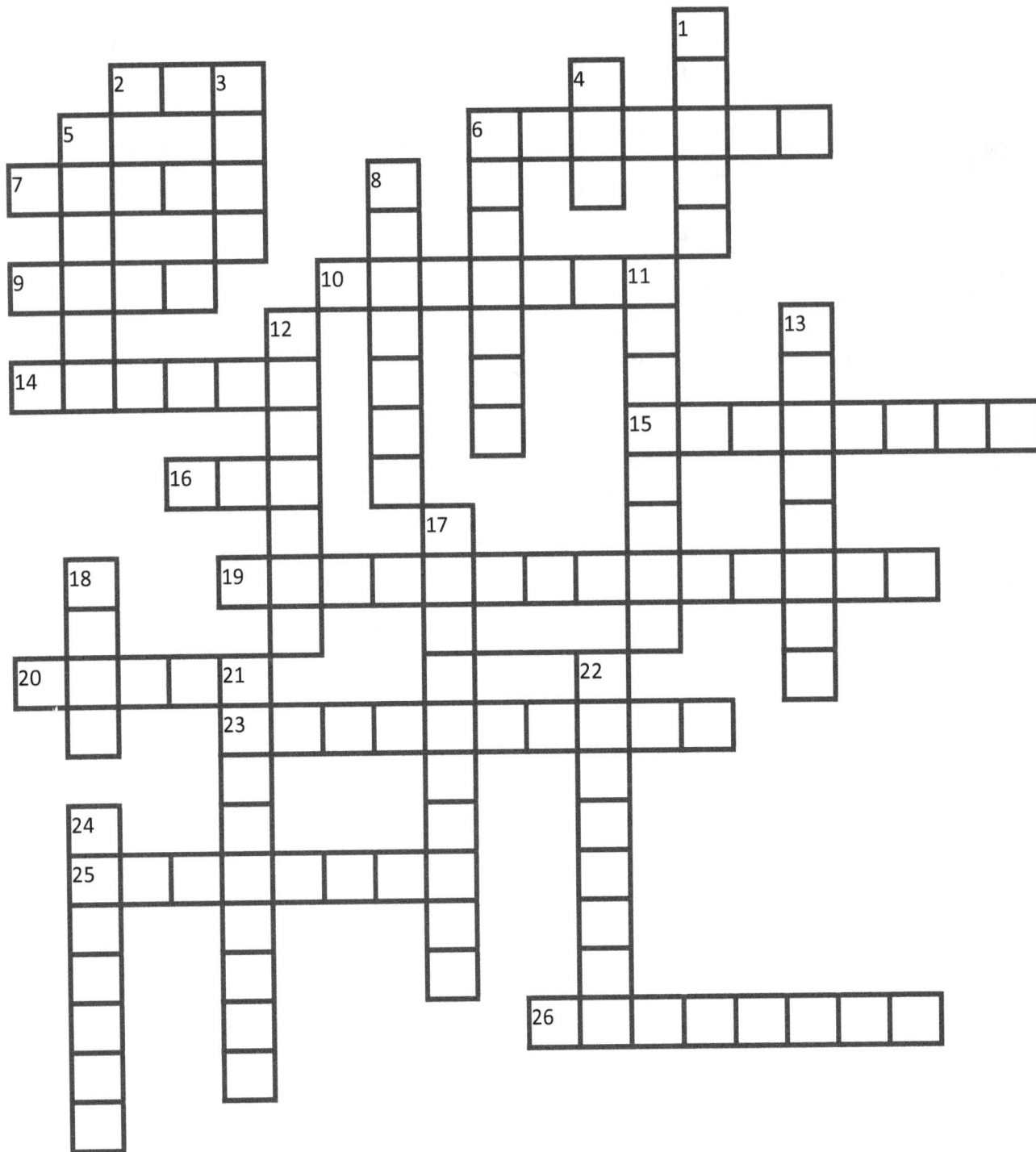

ADD
AREA
CUBE
DATA
DIFFERENCE
DIGIT
DIVISION
EQUAL

EQUATION
EXPRESSION
FACTORS
FEWER
FRACTION
HEXAGON
INFINITE
LENGTH

MINUTE
MULTIPLICATION
PATTERN
PRODUCT
QUARTER
RECTANGLE
RHOMBUS
ROW

SUBTRACT
SUM
TRIANGLE

	Across		**Down**
2.	To combine; put together two or more quantities.	1.	Having the same amount.
6.	The answer when two or more numbers are multiplied together.	3.	A collection of information.
7.	Any of the symbols 0, 1, 2, 3, 4, 5, 6, 7, 8, or 9.	4.	An arrangement of numbers or objects from left to right.
9.	A box-shaped solid object that has six identical square faces.	5.	A period of 60 seconds.
10.	The numbers that are multiplied together to get an answer in a multiplication problem.	6.	Things that are arranged following a rule or rules.
14.	A measure of how long something is.	8.	One of four equal parts.
15.	A plane figure with 3 straight sides and 3 vertices.	11.	To take away; remove; compare.
16.	The answer to an addition problem.	12.	A 4-sided flat shape with straight sides where all sides have equal length.
19.	A mathematical operation where a number is added to itself a number of times.	13.	A part of a whole.
20.	Smaller quantity or amount.	17.	The result when one number is subtracted from another.
23.	A mathematical phrase without an equal sign.	18.	The size of a surface.
25.	A number sentence with an equal sign.	21.	A plane figure with 4 sides and 4 square vertices.
26.	Without an end.	22.	Splitting into equal parts or groups.
		24.	A plane figure with six straight sides and six vertices.

Measurement

De-scramble each word to decrypt the final message.

LEGTHN

    27   9

EGTIHH

    10   25

TEGWIH

            18

NIECHS

    20   11

CESMENTIRTE

        5   12

TEEF

   19

UCENO

 17   2

TURQA

   7

LAONGL

  14   15

RIELT

23

RGMA

4

UCP

13

MAMLIGLRI

24

NOT

8 21 16

PODNU

1   22 28

NONET

26   6

RAMLIOGK

3

Y			
	1	2	3

4	5	6	7	8	9	10	11	12

13	14	15	16	17	18

B	
19	

| | | | | | | | | | !
|---|---|---|---|---|---|---|---|---|
| 20 | 21 | 22 | 23 | 24 | 25 | 26 | 27 | 28 |

If you get stuck, hold this page facing a mirror to reveal the answer below:

Your Greatest Cannot Be Contained!

www.ingramcontent.com/pod-product-compliance
Lightning Source LLC
Chambersburg PA
CBHW081304040426

42452CB00014B/2641